Original title:
The Clover Compass

Copyright © 2025 Creative Arts Management OÜ
All rights reserved.

Author: Tobias Winslow
ISBN HARDBACK: 978-1-80567-006-3
ISBN PAPERBACK: 978-1-80567-086-5

## The Serendipity of Wandering

In meadows bright, I lost my way,
Chasing butterflies on a sunny day.
A twist of fate, a sign to heed,
Found a road made of clover seed.

Each step a giggle, each corner a cheer,
Grass tickles my toes, what a sight here!
The trees were giggling, the clouds looked down,
Said, 'You're the oddest explorer in town!'

## Lost in Leafy Reveries

Under emerald canopies, I sat so still,
Chatting with acorns, against my will.
They spoke of travels, oh what a tale!
Of squirrels on ships and fish in a pail.

As I drifted off, a bird flew by,
With a wink and a chirp, oh my oh my!
'Take this path,' it said with a caw,
'You'll find more mischief than you ever saw!'

## Nature's Map of Dreams

A leaf fell down, it whispered sweet,
Leading my feet in a skip and a beat.
A map of laughter drawn on the breeze,
With dragonflies dancing among the trees.

Each bend revealed a curious surprise,
A frog in a suit, wearing sunglasses, oh my!
It croaked, 'Where's the party? I'm here for the fun!'
The sun laughed back, 'You've already won!'

## **Revelations Beneath Fourfold Canopies**

Beneath the leaves, I found a throne,
A munching snail claimed it for his own.
'This kingdom's vast,' he declared with pride,
'With a crown made of clover, I'll be your guide!'

Twirling in circles, the flowers all grinned,
They danced to the music that soft winds had sinned.
In this leafy realm, where laughter is free,
I lost my map, but found my glee!

## Echoes of Fortune Amongst the Green

In a field where luck does bloom,
Three leaves dance, dispelling gloom.
With a wink and cheeky grin,
They plot mischief, let the fun begin.

They whisper tales of treasure quests,
As daisies giggle, sharing jest.
A snail with shades joins in the cheer,
His slow-motion hi-five brings good luck near.

The rabbits hop with rhythm fine,
Wearing hats, sipping on sweet wine.
They chase the sun, no care in sight,
While ladybugs buzz with sheer delight.

A sprite tricks gnomes with a sly little wink,
As frogs croak truths, and cats just blink.
With every step, they roam and prance,
In luck's embrace, they jig and dance.

## Nature's Guiding Aroma

In fields where daisies sway and sing,
A scent of mischief fills the spring.
Bumblebees buzz, with comedic grace,
They dance around, like they're in a race.

The fragrant herbs plan secret plots,
To tease the noses of nearby tots.
With giggles and sniffs, oh what a chase,
Nature's scents lead to a funny place.

## **Echoes of Earth's Blessings.**

In the woods where shadows play a tune,
The trees tell jokes beneath the moon.
Leaves laugh softly at squirrel pranks,
As rabbits gather for silly shanks.

The flowers chuckle, petals in a spin,
Each bloom a giggle, each bud a grin.
Nature's echoes make good cheer,
In every rustle, a joke appears.

## **Whispers of Four Leaves**

Four leaves whisper secrets, oh so sly,
They giggle as the clovers wave goodbye.
Wandering ants in tiny shoes,
Dance to the rhythm of nature's blues.

They share their tales with the nearest frog,
Who croaks in laughter, lost in the fog.
Each breezy chuckle fills the air,
With nature's whimsy, nothing is rare.

## Navigating by Nature's Guide

The sun winks down, a playful tease,
While squirrels plot with giggling ease.
The map is drawn with twigs and stones,
As laughter echoes from leafy tones.

With chuckling winds that twist and twirl,
Nature's compass sends minds in a whirl.
Every turn leads to new delight,
In the treasure of laughter, day and night.

## Beneath the Canopy of Hope

Under leaves, we twist and twirl,
A clumsy dance, in nature's swirl.
Chasing shadows, giggles rise,
Who knew maps hide in the skies?

Branches wave like friendly friends,
Leading us where laughter bends.
Squirrels chuckle, pause to stare,
Did we just find bliss out there?

## Fourfold Wisdom in the Wild

Four leaves whisper playful hints,
In quiet corners, where sunlight hints.
Wise old owls share a grin,
As we lose the map, but let fun begin.

Rabbits hop, with winks so sly,
They know the game; it's worth a try.
Hold our breath, take a leap,
In whimsical paths, memories seep.

## Directions from Nature's Heart

Nature chuckles, soft and round,
Points us gently to the ground.
Watch the clouds, they joke and play,
"Follow us, or get lost today!"

Trees have secrets, whispers loud,
Bouncing echoes through the crowd.
Laughter grows along the way,
As all our worries simply sway.

## Secrets Hidden in Leafy Shadows

In shadowed greens, the mischief brews,
Mischievous paths, we choose to lose.
Giggling fawns play peek-a-boo,
Tugging at hearts, and spirits too.

Beneath the boughs, our laughter's shared,
With twinkling eyes that show we dared.
No sign would lead, but who needs that?
In playful chaos, we find our mat!

## Enchanted in Emerald Paths

In a forest bright and lush,
Little critters start to rush.
They search for treasures, oh so small,
To find their fortune, one and all.

With tiny maps made of pure luck,
Every step, a silly pluck.
They giggle when they spy a clue,
A fleeting squirrel races through.

A frog leaps high with a mighty splash,
Hoping to find his golden stash.
But all he finds is sticky mud,
And laughs out loud with a big thud.

So off they roam, both friend and foe,
In shimmering fields where mishaps grow.
For in this maze of plants and winks,
Who needs a map when joy just stinks?

## Leafy Tokens of Fate

Beneath the trees, a dance unfolds,
Where grass is green and the sun beholds.
Coins of clover flutter about,
As friends all gather and twist about.

A turtle slow, a rabbit quick,
Bet on who will find the trick.
A dandelion sneezes in the breeze,
While everyone giggles and snorts with ease.

With peppermints, they plot and scheme,
A leaf-turned-fortune seems a dream.
But when they spin and tumble down,
Laughter reigns, not the frown crown.

They trade the leaves for wishes made,
While roots entangle in the glade.
The whims of nature, pure delight,
In playful chaos, hearts take flight.

## A Pilgrimage to Green Gratitude

On a journey through the endless green,
A snail in shades of fun is seen.
He carries hopes and dreams so light,
With silly tales that spark delight.

With friends beside him, they share a pie,
A pie of clover—a grand old try!
They dance around, their hearts so free,
Creating magic with every spree.

A goat joins in, with shoes so grand,
Tap dancing to a silly band.
They leap and twirl on legs so lame,
Grateful for each giggly game.

Through fields of fortune, they will roam,
In every whim, they find a home.
No treasure greater than glee unfurled,
In this wild and wacky world.

## Nature's Sacred Way

In gardens lush, where wonders start,
Nature's tricks tickle the heart.
A ladybug misplaced her way,
Now she's lost in a leafy fray.

A wise old owl with glasses thick,
Tells silly jokes—and they just stick.
With every quirk that nature makes,
A laughter here is what it takes.

The flowers giggle, and bees all hum,
While squirrels dance with a rattle drum.
Their silly secrets, they share with glee,
In this goofy place where all are free.

So take a stroll on this green ballet,
Where laughter echoes every day.
For nature's way is full of fun,
In every step, your joy's begun!

# The Emerald Map of Life

In a patch so green, I found my way,
With a leaf on my hat, I'd dance and sway.
Each turn I took, made laughter bloom,
Maps and giggles filled the room.

Count my lucky charms and all their glee,
A compass that leads, whimsically.
Directions that twist, spin, and twirl,
In the clover's embrace, life gives a whirl.

With every step, a new surprise,
Chasing rainbows under sunny skies.
Who knew the way could be such fun?
In the green fields, I've barely begun.

My map of life with a silly glow,
Navigating paths only I know.
Join me, friend, let's skip along,
With a compass of giggles, we can't go wrong.

## The Guiding Leaf Beneath the Sky

A leaf fell down, and I followed tight,
It whispered secrets in pure delight.
Round and round, in circles I'd dance,
In the clover's kindness, I'd take my chance.

"Turn left!" it urged, "And smile so wide!"
With each wrong turn, I took it in stride.
Giggles ensued, paths led me astray,
Who knew the journey was child's play?

Beside the brook, I made a splash,
Laughing at life as I made a dash.
A guiding leaf, with a wink and a grin,
Promising adventures for all to begin.

Under the sky, the laughter soared,
With a twist and a turn, I was never bored.
Lost in the fun, what a lovely ride,
Thanks to that leaf, my trusty guide.

## Destined to Wander in Green Meadows

In meadows bright, I twirled and spun,
Wandering aimlessly, just for fun.
Clover companions, they danced with me,
In their outrageous antics, pure jubilee.

Each step a flop, each leap absurd,
Chasing butterflies, laughter stirred.
"Where to next?" I'd laugh and shout,
In this green sea, there's never a doubt.

A leap over daisies, a skip across streams,
Life is just better with silly dreams.
Every twist and turn, a giggle released,
In this silly ballet, worries decreased.

So here I march, my heart full of cheer,
With every clover, I'm drawn near.
Destined to wander, in meadows so fine,
A comical quest, in every line.

## **Four Folioed Directions of Destiny**

With four leaves bright, spun tales of fate,
I pondered the directions, not a moment late.
North, south, east, or a silly west,
All paths lead to laughs, life's very best.

One leaf's a giggle, another a cheer,
With such guidance, I have naught to fear.
"Just follow the fun!" they seem to say,
In the clover fields, I'd play all day.

Giddy in circles, dancing with glee,
Every turn I took led right back to me.
Lost in the laughter, found in delight,
With the four leaves' wisdom, life feels just right.

So grab your compass, let's wander wide,
In the meadows, we'll take a wild ride.
With each step forward, the world's a jest,
And a clovered path brings out the best.

## The Mapless Journey

Two friends set out with glee,
Lost on paths, who could foresee?
They followed squirrels, they followed bees,
Chasing laughter through the trees.

A treasure map with silly clues,
Points to places they'd never choose.
Found a picnic of ants and brie,
Who knew snacks were a mystery?

In their hearts, a grand quest blooms,
Instead of gold, they found balloon rooms.
And on a hill, they danced with sheep,
Their mapless journey made them leap.

Between the giggles, the fun unfolds,
Through grassy patches, boldness holds.
With each misstep, they'd laugh so loud,
Together in joy, forever proud.

## **Fortune's Gentle Breeze**

A gentle breeze blew through the park,
Tickling noses, igniting a spark.
It carried wishes, dreams galore,
While the pigeons plotted their next score.

They tossed a penny into a fountain,
Hoping for fortune to flow like a mountain.
But instead of gold, they caught a sock,
With unmatched style, the laughter would rock.

Mismatched dreams danced on the air,
Fortune's humor was everywhere.
As they chased butterflies, a kite took flight,
In silly moments, they found delight.

With every gust, the luck would spin,
In their hearts, the real treasure within.
For in friendship's embrace, they felt so free,
Just like fortune's gentle, breezy decree.

## Unveiling Hidden Blessings

Beneath a rock, a surprise awaits,
A jar of jellybeans, oh what fate!
With wild colors and flavors to share,
Each taste a giggle, beyond compare.

They sought for riches in hidden nooks,
Instead found stories in old storybooks.
Through laughter, they learned to see,
That blessings hide where they can be free.

A ladybug danced on a leaf,
Bestowing cheer, what a relief!
In every crevice of playful cheer,
They unearthed joy that was crystal clear.

With every giggle and silly dance,
Hidden treasures made them prance.
For in the search, they found their bliss,
A bounty of fun in every twist.

## **Treading Through Gardened Dreams**

In a garden where whimsy grows,
A sunflower wearied by passing crows.
They tiptoed through petals, bright and bold,
Finding secrets only they could hold.

A bunny with glasses, reading all day,
Told stories of clouds that danced in May.
With each wild tale, their giggles soared,
In this lush land where dreams were stored.

They planted wishes with silly names,
A potato prince and a queen of flames.
With every sprout, a chuckle broke,
Treading their way through dreams bespoke.

In this garden, joy takes root,
Where laughter blooms, there's no dispute.
Through every path, they joyfully screamed,
In a world where laughter reigns, they dreamed.

## The Symphony of Wandering Leaves

Leaves drift down like confetti,
Twirling in a laughter spree.
Each gust of wind's a cheeky prank,
As they dance 'round the old oak plank.

Squirrels plot their acorn heist,
While birds have brunch, oh what a feast!
Gathering treasures with joyful cheer,
Nature's wacky volunteers!

Pine cones roll like merry balls,
Making music as the wind calls.
A swirl of colors, bright and bold,
Tales of mischief yet untold!

As autumn sings its comical tune,
Even the mushrooms join the swoon.
With every step, we trip and laugh,
In nature's wild and silly path.

## **The Cartographer of Green Dreams**

Maps are drawn with leaves and paws,
X marks the spot for giggled jaws.
With every twist and every turn,
We chart the fun that we still yearn.

A snail's pace could be a race,
With butterflies adding to the chase.
Rocky roads are worth the bumpy ride,
Especially with friends right by your side.

Upside-down maps from tree to tree,
A compass of laughter, wild and free.
Get lost in joy, it's our grand scheme,
Navigating through our daydream.

We find the hidden wells of glee,
In every leaf, in every tree.
Who knew a stroll could lead to grace,
In a world that's just a funny place?

## Pathways Under the Cover of Leaves

Under a canopy of smiles so wide,
The ground holds secrets that roll and slide.
A path made of giggles and trails so bright,
Feels like an adventure, pure delight!

A rabbit hops with a jaunty stride,
While hedgehogs hide and kittens abide.
Each critter's got a story or two,
Of mischief, laughter, and wacky woo-hoo.

Step over roots that want to trip,
Laugh at the puddles that make you slip.
With every twist over a leaf-strewn lane,
You'll find joy in every little gain.

Through tangled vines, our giggles ring,
From every corner, the forest sings.
Join the parade, step lively and brave,
In our world of whimsy, we all misbehave!

# Nature's Directions from Above

Clouds roll by with a giggly grin,
Pointing directions where our fun begins.
Rainbows curve like a rainbow hook,
Taking us where the whimsy is booked.

Birds tweet codes in a language so silly,
A map where joy is the only frilly.
With sunbeams shining, giving a wink,
Follow the glow, don't stop to think!

Stars sprinkle wisdom from nights that fly,
As critters march under the watchful sky.
Each moment mapped with laughter and cheer,
In nature's playground, we have no fear.

So gaze above, let your spirit roam,
In loops of joy, nature feels like home.
With funny signs that make us giggle,
We'll dance along and happiness wiggle!

## **Signs of Solace in the Tangle**

In a twisty maze of green, I roam,
With laughing leaves that call me home.
A squirrel dances, makes me grin,
While weeds decide who'll be my kin.

A garden gnome gives me a wink,
As dandelions start to sink.
I chuckle at their stubborn plight,
Their lofty dreams are quite a sight.

I trip on roots and start to sway,
The map I hold has gone astray.
But in this laughter, I find my way,
Through tangled paths of bright array.

So here in knots, I lose my frown,
The silly greens won't let me down.
With every step, I play my song,
In joy, I find where I belong.

## Lucky Directions Under the Moon

Beneath the moon's soft, glowing light,
I navigate with laughter bright.
A rabbit points with a friendly paw,
As mischief hides within the straw.

The stars are giggling up above,
While fireflies twinkle, light their love.
I follow trails of spark and cheer,
Where every shadow whispers near.

The wind, it teases like a friend,
And tells me tales that never end.
With every turn, a giggle's heard,
As wishes scatter like a bird.

So off I hop, with steps so light,
The path ahead is pure delight.
In this adventure, joy's the key,
As I chase luck, wild and free.

# From Green to Gold: A Traveler's Guide

Through fields of green, I glide and sway,
Collecting laughter as I play.
Along the way, a sign appears,
It's covered thick in gopher sneers.

A ladybug gives me directions,
While bees provide the best connections.
"Just follow us!" they buzz and hum,
In this silly dance, I feel the fun.

I tumble on the golden grass,
As clumsy critters watch me pass.
With every slip, I'm born anew,
In perfect paths of green and dew.

So here's my guide to fun and cheer,
Embrace the breezes drawing near.
With each sweet step, I lose control,
Yet find a treasure in my soul.

## Seeking Harmony in Leafy Silence

Amidst the hush of leafy trees,
I seek the harmony of glee.
A chipmunk chirps, gives me a clue,
That nature's laughter sings so true.

With every step through branches wide,
I feel the chuckles swell inside.
A whisper tickles at my ear,
As flowers giggle, "Join us here!"

The sun dips low, a golden smile,
I wander freely, mile by mile.
Each stumble brings a silly cheer,
For silly slips just draw me near.

In leafy silence, joy takes flight,
I roam with creatures of pure light.
A funny dance beneath the trees,
In nature's arms, I feel such ease.

## **Fortune's Leafy Signpost**

In a garden dense and spry,
A leaf once whispered, oh my!
With a wink and a twisty leaf,
It promised fortune, what a relief!

Through patches green, a path to tread,
With giggles and jokes, I was led.
A signpost here, its leaves all jive,
Navigating luck, I felt so alive!

Underneath blooms, a map unfolds,
Tales of mischief, adventure bold.
When the sun shines, my compass grins,
Pointing to joy, where laughter begins!

So follow along, dear wandering friend,
With each silly twist, around every bend.
The leafy guide's always just right,
In this garden of giggles, pure delight!

# Green Paths and Hidden Signs

Wandering paths of emerald hue,
I stumbled on signs with a giggling crew.
Each leaf pointed with a chuckle and cheer,
Leading me to mischief, oh dear!

Laughter echoes where secrets lie,
Among the foliage, oh me, oh my!
The signs that giggle, with voices so bright,
Take me to wonders, pure delight!

In the midst of clovers, I found a dance,
A jig and a twirl, what a funny chance!
Each step I took, the ground did reply,
With tickles and grins, I felt I could fly!

So join me dear friend, let's not be shy,
Let's wander the paths where the leafy laughs lie.
In this realm of jests, a lucky sign,
We'll frolic and play, holding fortune divine!

## The Wayfinder's Fourfold Tale

Once in a meadow, bright as a meme,
A wayfinder's journey turned into a dream.
With every step, the grass had a quirk,
Each turn revealed a silly perk!

A twist of fate, a follow of signs,
And luck danced 'round like playful vines.
Every fork in the trail made me cackle,
With each silly misstep, I started to crackle!

A leafy compass with secrets to share,
Guiding my way through the mischief laid bare.
With giggles and guffaws, I spun in delight,
Finding riches of laughter all day and all night!

So heed my tale, of paths often bent,
With fortune in laughter, your worries are spent.
For in the grassy giggles, the mischief resides,
In this leafy labyrinth, joy always abides!

## Trails of the Lucky Foliage

Along the trails where green curls play,
I chased after giggles, brightening my day.
A rustle of leaves, a wink from a vine,
Every step I took felt like drinking fine wine!

Hidden treasures beneath each clump,
The foliage danced, giving each leaf a thump.
With laughter as our guide, so bold and bright,
Every twist in our tales brought pure delight!

The signs of fortune, all green and spry,
Lead us to chuckles, oh let out a sigh!
The journey's the worth, not the coin or the prize,
Just follow the giggles, under starlit skies!

So frolic with me, through paths verdant and wild,
In this leafy journey, let's come back, like a child.
The maps we'll unfurl, with much laughter to see,
For in this adventure, forever be free!

## Journeying Through Nature's Embrace

In fields of green where daisies dance,
The bees play tag, a buzzing chance.
We follow paths of slippery mud,
Laughing as we trip with a thud.

The sun above, a jester bright,
Tossing beams left and right.
Napping under a leafy crown,
Dreams of squirrels and acorns abound.

## **The Whimsy of Wandering Leaves**

Oh, how the leaves make quite the show,
Twirling down like they know where to go.
One took a dive straight into my hat,
Declaring, "This is where I'll chat!"

They giggle and swirl in the autumn breeze,
Whispering tales of pies and cheese.
Chasing a breeze, they tumble and play,
Who knew nature could be so cliché?

## Navigating Life's Gentle Currents

A stream serenades with a bubbly tune,
Inviting us over for a picnic at noon.
Where fish wear hats and frogs wear shoes,
All while I feast on snacks I can't refuse!

Rafts of leaves float by like boats,
Sailing high on the dreams of goats.
Our laughter carries on the winding way,
As we navigate folly, come what may.

## The Language of Leaves and Turns

Scribbles of green in a sunny hue,
Let's decipher their language, me and you.
A leaf pokes fun, "Try over there!"
As I stumble and roll down with flair.

With each twist and turn, giggles accrue,
As branches snap jokes that are silly but true.
In this leafy world, we lose track of time,
Every step a verse, every laugh a rhyme.

## Under the Shade of Leafy Legends

Beneath the leaves, tales unfold,
Where giggles sprout, the brave and bold.
A garden gnome looks quite confused,
His salad's lost, his dreams misused.

The squirrels dance in their little hats,
While frogs croak songs to the chubby cats.
The ladybugs have all called a truce,
With ants who claim they're the best at juice.

In shadows, whispers of mischief flow,
As snails hold races, but move too slow.
The breeze tells secrets, old and spry,
Of lovers who lost their keys and cried.

So, grab your hat and join the crew,
For magic here is silly and true.
Under this shade, let laughter bloom,
And paint our lives to chase away gloom.

## The Serenity of Lucky Trails

On paths so green, we find delight,
With quirky critters that dance at night.
A snail named Gus wears glittery shoes,
He twirls and slips in his fancy blues.

We spot a rabbit who can't stop prance,
His carrots lost in a funny dance.
A turtle races, but oh, how slow!
He's holding up a traffic show!

A feathered friend sings off-key tunes,
Where daisies sway and wildflowers croon.
Each step unveils a jester's tune,
As nature joins in this comic swoon.

By the babbling brook, we plop and stare,
At fish who giggle without a care.
With smiles so big, they leap and glide,
In this serene silliness, we all reside.

## Wandering Between Verdant Whispers

In leafy realms where whispers laugh,
A quirky frog just lost his path.
He hops along with flair and style,
While other critters pause and smile.

A snake in shades thinks it's a deck,
While pretending to be a shipwrecked speck.
An owl with glasses reads a map,
But can't decide—should he take a nap?

The flowers gossip in hues so bright,
About a spider with a fear of heights.
He's weaving dreams of the skies so wide,
While butterflies swirl and take a ride.

As the sun dips low, the mischief grows,
With gigging beetles and ticklish toes.
With laughter shared and tales to spin,
In this verdant playground, everyone wins.

# Leafy Labyrinths and Hidden Paths

In tangled trails, we wander free,
Where every turn is a mystery.
A duck in boots quacks out a rhyme,
Claiming to have discovered lime.

The hedgehogs smile with prickly pride,
While beetles march in a silly stride.
The mushrooms host a tea party grand,
With tarts made by a wobbly hand.

Over hills and through glades we roam,
Chasing laughter, we feel at home.
A lizard juggles and drops his flies,
As chipmunks giggle and roll their eyes.

Through leafy mazes and paths unknown,
Adventure lurks in every tone.
So take a step, let joy ignite,
In this whimsical world, everything's right.

## **Emerald Guiding Stars**

In fields so bright, the greens hold sway,
Where four-leaved wonders dance and play.
A compass points, or so they claim,
But grass grows wild, and I feel no shame.

With giggles loud, I start to roam,
Searching for luck in my leafy home.
Each step I take, I skip and twirl,
In this strange land, it's a lucky whirl.

A rabbit hops with a wink and grin,
Saying, "Life's a game, come join in!"
I scan the ground for gems of lore,
Where bushes hide magical lore galore.

Through tangled reeds and dandy fluff,
They say good fortune just seems tough.
But as I laugh and chase my fate,
Every green leaf, I truly appreciate.

## Seeking Shelter Under Four Leaves

Beneath the sky, so wide and blue,
I hunt for luck—that's what I do.
With four leaves found, I'll dodge the rain,
And look like royalty in leafy reign.

A squirrel debates what nut to share,
While asking me why I care.
"To find a treasure beneath this tree,
And maybe dance with the lucky spree!"

Here comes a flower, all dressed in cheer,
It's singing songs for all to hear.
"Bounce along and join my tune,
You'll leave your worries by afternoon!"

As shadows lengthen and laughter flows,
I smile at every creature that knows.
For under green, my worries cease,
In this crazy hunt, I find my peace.

## Enchanted Waypoints in the Meadow

In a meadow bright, where flowers prance,
I chase my luck with a playful dance.
Each twirl and leap, a new surprise,
Where even daisies can claim the prize.

A ladybug smiles, perched on a leaf,
Spreading bustling joy beyond belief.
"Come find the map!" it seems to tease,
As I tumble and roll with effort to please.

Now ants parade in their tiny shoes,
With a plan so grand, they can't refuse.
"Join our quest, you'll surely see,
While searching for leaves, just be carefree!"

As day turns bright then fades from view,
Under starlit skies, I find my crew.
In leafy paths where giggles soar,
Adventure waits behind every door.

## The Journey of Fortune's Foliage

Starting off on a whimsy quest,
To find that luck, I think I'm blessed.
With every step, I hope to score,
The merry leaves are never a bore.

Behind a bush, a fox appears,
With shiny eyes and a grin that cheers.
"Join my party, don't be shy,
We'll uncover luck and wonders nearby!"

Through lilac blooms and twinkling grass,
We dance along as time goes fast.
I count the leaves and share my dreams,
On this playful route, laughter streams.

As dusk arrives, we end the spree,
Fortune found, in hearts so free.
With friends by side, we'll keep it real,
In this wild world, so much appeal!

## **Overgrown Roads Less Traveled**

Down the lane where weeds grow high,
I found a tire swing, oh my!
With squirrels cheering, I took a leap,
Landing in a patch of sheep!

Grasshoppers danced, wearing hats so neat,
While ants rehearsed a marching beat.
Backpacks stuffed with snacks galore,
Explorers laugh as they hit the floor!

Laughter echoes in this wild escape,
With muddy shoes, and a twisted cape.
We map the trails with silly drawings,
Chasing squirrels and other misdoings!

Adventure calls with a jolly cheer,
In paths unmarked, no worry or fear.
Take that route where chaos reigns,
And cherish the joy this madness contains!

## Green Traces of Forgotten Journeys

Once upon a trail of green,
I hopped on stones, a sight unseen.
Mossy feet and giggles bright,
Chasing fireflies into the night.

Cabbage patches waved hello,
As we took turns in a row.
My friend tripped, fell in a patch,
And came up with a leafy batch!

Old maps made of spaghetti strings,
Led us to the silliest things.
We found a treasure, quite absurd,
A rubber duck? A singing bird?

With every twist and every bend,
These green traces make us blend.
We'll laugh and wander till we tire,
In fields of fun, we will conspire!

# A Quest for Nature's Synchronicity

Bumblebees wore tiny hats,
As we quested for the chattiest chats.
In sync, we hopped and twirled with glee,
While flowers giggled, green as can be.

Rabbits in bowties joined our spree,
Leading us to a raucous tree.
We sang with birds, a funny tune,
Until we accidentally woke the moon!

Nature's rhythm felt so right,
Even frogs began to dance in flight.
With every step, new laughter grew,
In this zany meeting, joy just flew!

Our adventure's song, a playful cheer,
Echoes of laughter for all to hear.
In each step, we find our beat,
On this quest, life feels so sweet!

## The Leafy Path and Starry Skies

On a leafy path where giggles bloom,
We found some shrooms with a little room.
Dancing mushrooms sang a tune,
While owls hooted under the moon.

Starry skies winked with delight,
As raccoons held a party all night.
With twinkling snacks and silly hats,
We joined the fun with silly chats!

Under trees that twisted high,
We leaped for stars, oh my, oh my!
The squirrels rolled by in a cartwheel race,
As laughter echo in this nutty place.

So grab your snacks and bring your cheer,
In this leafy realm, there's nothing to fear.
Let's dance among the shadows and glow,
In this whimsical party, let the fun flow!

## A Journey Through Verdant Hues

In fields so green, we roam the land,
With petal hats and clover bands.
We search for luck with silly grins,
Yet find more joy in dandelion sins.

Each step we take, the leaves do chuckle,
As we trip on roots, what a fine shuffle!
Two left feet on a grassy runner,
This journey's fun, who needs to be a winner?

Among the charm of buzzing bees,
We dance a jig, just aim to please.
With every hop, the grass-tips tease,
Oh, how we laugh in this leafy breeze!

The sun sets low, our antics done,
We'll call it a day, a day so fun!
With memories green, and hearts so light,
We dream of dance till the stars ignite.

## Navigating Life's Green Maze

We find ourselves in a maze of greens,
Chasing dreams like silly gleaners.
With paper maps that make no sense,
We shrug, and smile, it's all pretense!

A squirrel guides with a twitchy tail,
As we follow pathways that seem to fail.
With branches swaying, laughing loud,
We wear our confusion like a proud shroud.

Turn left, turn right, or just stand still,
Who needs a map when there's time to kill?
We take each twist with a playful tease,
And giggle as nature puts us at ease.

With each wrong turn, the sun dips low,
We dance through clovers, letting life flow.
A maze of green, with giggles in tow,
In this wacky world, our spirits grow.

## Leafy Directions and Wandering Souls

Two wandering souls with leafy hats,
We bumble through grass, dodging the cats.
With a compass made of twigs and dreams,
We follow our laughter, at least it seems!

A signpost sways, it points to fun,
We skip right past, chasing the sun.
With giggles bursting like pollen in June,
We dance with ferns, a whimsical tune.

We toss aside our paths so straight,
As leaves conspire to change our fate.
With every step, mischief brews,
Boundaries blur in this world of dew.

We wander forth, with chatter and cheer,
In nature's grasp, there's nothing to fear.
With wandering souls and dreams untold,
In the leafy embrace, we find our gold.

## The Compass of Nature's Gifts

In the woods where laughter sings,
Our compass spins, with silly flings.
A map of leaves, and giggles galore,
Who needs directions when we've got lore?

A twisty path, just follow the quack,
A duck leads the way, no fear of flack.
With every step and hop we take,
We find the joy in every mistake!

The trees join in, with whispers of fun,
A game of tag, under the sun.
With nature's gifts in silly disarray,
We play till dusk, pushed worries away.

With every stumble, there's laughter to win,
Our hearts map out where the giggles begin.
From frog leaps to twirls, we follow the lift,
In this merry dance, we discover nature's gift.

## In Search of Treasured Fields

Beneath a sky of floppy hats,
I hunt for greens where fortune chats.
A patch of luck, or so they say,
But it just leads me far astray.

With friends who giggle and point out finds,
I tumble over clovers, tangled in vines.
A treasure map of silly dreams,
I end up just counting ants and streams.

A ladybug dances, full of flair,
In a field that's buzzing, without a care.
My compass spins, oh what a trip!
Who knew the grass could be such a whip?

Still, I hold heartily onto my quest,
For luck must be hiding, it's just a jest.
The roly-poly rolls near my shoe,
"Found it!" I shout, my luck's coming true!

## Labyrinth of Leafy Luck

In a jungle of green, where clovers play,
I wander and spin, like a child at sway.
Each turn a giggle, each step a flip,
In search of a fortune, on this wild trip.

A beetle scuttles, a dance on the ground,
With roots like mazes, I'm happily bound.
But where is the exit? I question my path,
With leafy laughter, it's all a good math.

I twist and I turn, like a circus clown,
Through clover jungles and grassy towns.
It seems my fortune's gone on a spree,
Hiding in giggles, not found by me!

Then suddenly there, a four-leaf sight,
I pluck it with glee, what a delight!
Yet, the moment I turn, who do I see?
A squirrel laughing, he's taken the glee!

## Compass Points in Nature's Embrace

A compass points in circles tight,
While I'm distracted by a butterfly's flight.
My map is soggy from the morning dew,
But laughter in clovers is never askew.

With each little step, my path goes round,
Only to trip over roots in the ground.
Exploring the greens with a jesting heart,
Finding my fortune, a comedic art!

"True north" says my friend, confused in glee;
While munching on clovers, with honeyed tea.
The compass, it giggles, and points with flair,
To a picnic party where no one can care.

We nibble on luck, every leaf a bite,
With treats aplenty, what a silly sight!
So we toast to greens, in the sun's warm glow,
For laughter's true treasure is all that we know!

## Mystical Greens of Guidance

In dreamy meadows, where luck may dwell,
I dance with breezes, casting my spell.
With twinkling eyes, I seek the sign,
But end up chasing shadows that play and recline.

"Pick a leaf!" my buddies call with glee,
I pluck and I poke, "Is this lucky me?"
A patch of green is a whimsical tease,
Until I find ants serving tiny keys!

With every turn, there's a chuckling breeze,
Whispering secrets of giggles and tease.
I'm twirled around by the dandelion's chains,
And what was confusion is laughter that reigns!

Yet, after adventures of green and gold,
I've stocked up on stories and laughter untold.
So here's to the quest, with a joyful heart,
For every slippery clover is a laugh to impart!

## **Secrets in the Meadow's Heart**

In fields where whispers twine and dance,
The oddest things may just enhance.
A rabbit wears a tiny hat,
And giggles at a chatty cat.

Beneath the blooms, a secret plays,
With bees who buzz in wacky ways.
They dance like clowns in silly shoes,
Stealing sips of morning dew.

A turtle dreams of running fast,
While mice are playing cards, amassed.
The daisies gossip, oh so spry,
Of all the dreams that float on by.

## Journeys Through Verdant Fortune

A squirrel claims the tallest perch,
Proclaiming he's the king of mirth.
With acorn crown and twiggy throng,
He leads a parade, all day long.

Along the path where green things grow,
A cactus joins, but moves too slow.
It points the way with spiky care,
While rabbits hop without a care.

They find a patch where giggles bloom,
And mushrooms play a jaunty tune.
With every step, they find surprise,
Beneath the sun, the world complies.

## The Pathway of Promise

Two ants embarked on bold, bright quest,
To find the fruit that's simply best.
With tiny maps and giggles loud,
They vowed to make their families proud.

But paths got tangled, twists and turns,
Where every leaf had tricks to learn.
A worm performed a magic trick,
And made the journey feel quite slick.

They stumbled on a picnic spread,
With crumbs enough to feed a shed.
A song of laughter filled the air,
As critters danced without a care.

## **Symbols of Serenity**

A ladybug with polka dots,
Declared itself a prince, not just lots.
In tiny courts of buttercups,
It ruled over flower cups.

With tea made from the morning dew,
And tales of skies in shades of blue.
A dandelion made a wish,
To fly away and dance like this.

## Glide the Forest's Gentle Path

Beneath the trees we lie in wait,
For squirrels to gossip, then debate.
They chatter loud, a wild brigade,
While we just grin, in sunlit shade.

A dandelion stops to dance,
Inviting bees to take a chance.
They buzz around, a sticky crew,
And steal our picnic, just like that, boo-hoo!

With each twig snap a story unfolds,
Of epic battles, of heroes bold.
We cheer them on, though they can't see,
Our laughter echoed through the trees.

And when the shadows start to creep,
We find that nature likes to keep
A secret stash of jokes and jests,
In every leaf, it surely rests.

## Voyages Through Verdant Newness

In fields of green we roam and bound,
Where grasshoppers leap, making sound.
They sing of mischief, bold and wild,
While muddy toes are nature's child.

Mushrooms sprout like little hats,
And hide from us, those merry brats.
We poke and prod, they giggle back,
'Catch us if you can!' they quack.

Butterflies lead a waltz through air,
Flirting with flowers, without a care.
They flutter, tease, then twist and swirl,
As we take turns in this leafy whirl.

The sun dips low, we stretch and sigh,
Saying goodnight to the bugs that fly.
With twinkling stars our guide through the night,
We'll laugh 'til dawn in the soft twilight.

## Hidden in the Embrace of Nature

Among the roots where secrets lie,
A frog in a bow tie jumps up high.
He croaks about his posh affair,
As ladybugs giggle, without a care.

In this green maze the wild things play,
Throwing wild parties, come what may.
With acorns dropping like confetti rain,
We join the fun, without disdain.

A wise old owl, with spectacles round,
Tells tales of the mischief he's found.
We nod and chuckle, for who could resist,
A sage with whimsy in a world like this?

Fireflies join in with their bright light,
Creating a glow that feels just right.
We dance among shadows, feeling quite spry,
In nature's embrace, we laugh and fly.

## Secrets of the Growling Ground

In gardens where the gnomes take charge,
We find some mysteries, oh so large.
The ground grumbles like a hungry beast,
While rabbits sip tea, not the least a feast.

Petunias gossip, flaunting their hues,
About the rumors of garden shoes.
We snicker and sneer, join the parade,
As garden tools form a masquerade.

The wind playfully tugs at our hats,
While worms conspire, sharing their spats.
They wriggle with laughter, they've got the moves,
Creating tangoes where nobody snooze.

As twilight draws near with a yawn and a sigh,
We gather the stories, one last goodbye.
In whispers of leaves and the hum of the ground,
We leave with a chuckle of joy all around.

## Whispers of Luck

In a garden of greens so bright,
A tale of chance takes flight.
A ladybug wearing a hat,
Tips the scales with a little chat.

With a jig and a wiggle, he struts,
Rolling dice in tiny ruts.
A four-leaf party ensues,
As squirrels debate the latest news.

A rabbit hops with a wink,
Proposing a toast to the drink.
The grass sings a chime,
As luck dances, feeling prime.

So here's to whispers, soft and clear,
A world where fortune draws near.
In this quirky garden live,
The secret to how luck can thrive.

## Four Leaves of Destiny

In a patch where mischief thrives,
Four leaves twist, and luck arrives.
A clumsy cat in search of cream,
Tripped on fate, or so it seemed.

A lizard wearing shades of green,
Suns himself, a luck machine.
With tales of dance and playful jive,
He spins around, oh what a dive!

With each turn comes a giggle,
Fate tickles like a quickened wiggle.
The odds may dance and whims may sway,
But who knows what the dice will play?

So raise a glass to what may be,
In this garden, wild and free.
Four leaves twist and swirl so spry—
Hop on luck, it's worth a try!

## **Serendipity's Guide**

There's a map made of green delight,
With arrows drawn in joyful flight.
It leads to adventures, oh so wacky,
Where rabbits wear coats and don't feel tacky.

A mischievous squirrel, with a plan,
Juggles acorns, a real-life fan.
His compass spins, a dizzy tale,
While ducks in bow ties set their sail.

In this land of unexpected quests,
Even mushrooms wear their festive vests.
Each twist yields a chuckle or two,
As luck pings like a game that's new.

So follow the guide, don't lag behind,
In every stumble, joy you'll find.
With serendipity in full swing,
It's a mad dash to the next lucky fling!

## Beneath the Lucky Shade

Under branches with ideas bright,
Where shadows dance with pure delight.
A wise old gnome, he tells a joke,
While flowers blush in laughter's smoke.

Each petal flutters, a giggling theme,
In the rays of chance, they truly beam.
A beetle wearing a tiny bow,
Claims the luckiest spot in the show.

The clouds drift in a silly mood,
Raindrops play hide and seek, oh dude!
While butterflies flit with vibrant flair,
Chasing the echoes of laughter in air.

So sit beneath this shaded tree,
Where fortune whispers joyfully.
In this funny glade, come play along,
For luck thrives in a light-hearted song!

## In Search of the Green Infinity

In a patch where luck does sprout,
I lost my route, with twist and shout.
The leaves winked back, what a sight,
As I danced with joy, oh what a fright!

The grass giggled, tickling my knees,
While daisies joined in, swaying with ease.
I asked a worm for advice on my quest,
It just wiggled away, I must've impressed!

Searching for fortune 'neath the sun's beam,
I tripped over roots, still chasing my dream.
With each silly stumble, the laughter grew,
Who knew bad luck could lead me to you?

I found a four-leaf clover today,
But my dog snatched it right away!
Now I'm left here with a grin so wide,
'Cause my pup's the luckiest one, I can't hide!

# The Enigma of Leafy Pathways

On a leafy road where secrets lie,
I questioned a frog, who just waved bye.
The trees were gossiping, couldn't you hear?
Their whispers tickled me, bringing good cheer.

I followed a squirrel, thought it was wise,
He led me in circles, oh what a surprise!
Chasing my tail, I spun like a top,
Like leaves in the wind, I couldn't stop!

A dandelion puff offered its aid,
But fluttered away, my plans delayed.
I sat on a bench beside a wise ant,
Who scribbled my fortune—turns out I can't!

Yet the laughter of nature made it all fine,
Even when butterflies skipped the straight line.
Through twisty pathways, I finally found,
That joy in the journey is luck that's profound!

## Fortunate Steps on Gentle Trails

Upon gentle trails, where the daisies play,
I realized fortune was just a skip away.
With each step I took, the path seemed to giggle,
Even the rocks started doing a wiggle!

A ladybug waved, as if she could see,
The potential for fun in my foolish spree.
I asked for good luck, and what did I get?
A shower of pollen, now what a pet!

The breeze turned to music, it carried my plight,
As grasshoppers chirped, oh what a delight!
Each jump filled with laughter, swirls in the air,
In my odd little adventure, I really don't care.

Through bumps and through giggles, I stumbled along,
The journey was silly, and nature's my song.
With a heart full of joy and a head full of dreams,
I danced with the leaves, how funny it seems!

## Messages Weaving Through Nature's Thread

Whispers of leaves weave tales so bright,
Messages floating like birds in flight.
I stopped for a chat with a curious fern,
Who giggled at secrets I wished to learn.

A butterfly fluttered, with wisdom to share,
But then got distracted by her own flair.
In the maze of green, I got hopelessly lost,
Wrapped up in laughter, forgetting the cost.

A breeze tossed my hat into a tree,
Where a raccoon mocked me, a sight to see!
While I climbed for my treasure, the laughter grew loud,
For nature's a jester, a whimsical crowd.

So here's to the mishaps, the giggles we'll keep,
In this tapestry made, we often take leaps.
Every message unspooled, a joy for the heart,
In the funny adventures, we all play a part.

## Lost Among the Echoes of Green

In the meadow where shadows play,
Four leaves dance in a silly sway.
I trip on roots, then start to hum,
As daisies giggle, 'Here he comes!'

A squirrel mocks with acorn in hand,
While butterflies paint the flower band.
I shout, "Map me out, you leafy crew!"
But all they do is wink and skew.

Chasing circles, I stumble and fall,
Grass stains proudly, oh what a ball!
With whispers loud from the trees above,
They tease my quest for luck and love.

Yet in the chaos, I find my way,
Through paths of clovers where laughter stay.
With each step on this quirky spree,
I'm lost, but joyfully, you see!

## The Map of Nature's Mysteries

Beneath the stars, I squint and stare,
Mapping wonders in the cool night air.
An owl hoots as if giving clues,
But all I find are thorny shoes.

A raccoon giggles, peeking near,
"Your treasure map is really quite queer!"
I scribble notes on a leaf with glee,
While fireflies buzz, as if to tease me.

The rivers chuckle, the mountains roll,
Their rocky laughter takes quite a toll.
I stumble upon a bubbling brook,
Wondering if moss can read a book.

Exploring twists with a crooked grin,
Adventures sparked as the night wears thin.
With every mystery, a silly tale,
Nature's map leads me down the trail!

## Beneath the Fourfold Secret Canopy

Under arches of leaves so wide,
Secret giggles I cannot hide.
A fox in specs reads the news,
As mushrooms tease with patterned views.

Branches bend like a ticklish brat,
Whispering secrets to every chat.
I shake my head, confusion abounds,
Why do thorns make the silliest sounds?

In this forest, I'm the punchline too,
Getting lost is what I always do.
But ferns are kind and sprout their wings,
While the laughter of chipmunks softly sings.

And though I may wander and stray,
Each corner turned brings a bright display.
Under this canopy, a whimsical spree,
I find joy where the wild things be!

## A Compass of Dreams and Leaves

With dreams in pockets, I roam the glade,
A compass that spins in a leafy parade.
The groundhog points with a cheeky grin,
"This way to fun! Let the laughs begin!"

A toad on a lily keeps score of laughs,
While rabbits duel in absurdity staffs.
With laughter echoing from leafy seams,
I follow the path of ridiculous dreams.

The sun peeks out from the trees so tall,
Chasing shadows that flicker and fall.
Each step unveils a new joke or cheer,
As nature chuckles, my fears disappear.

So here I am, in this mischievous maze,
Finding joy in the quirkiest ways.
No compass true needed; just follow the sights,
For laughter blooms where the spirit ignites!

## Delving into Verdant Whispers

In a meadow where giggles grow,
A mischievous breeze starts to blow.
The clovers dance, what a silly sight,
They tickle the toes, oh what a delight!

With each little leaf, a secret unfolds,
Tales of pranks that the garden holds.
A rabbit in glasses, a frog in a tie,
Chasing the clouds as they float by.

Each step taken feels rather absurd,
The sunlight laughs, have you heard?
A ladybug winks with a wink so bold,
Whispering stories never told!

In this patch of green, joy takes flight,
Laughter bursts forth, oh what a sight!
Make a wish on a leaf that's spry,
And join the giggles beneath the sky!

## Signs of Serendipity

A signpost wobbles, what does it say?
'Follow your nose, the weird way!'
So off we trot, on this odd quest,
Hoping the clovers know what's best.

A squirrel wears a beret with flair,
He flips through the leaves as if with care.
Perhaps he's a guide, or just quite lost,
But we follow his lead, no matter the cost.

Each clover we find could lead us to fun,
Like ice cream castles or a hot dog run!
We chase after shadows, we leap with glee,
For this silly journey is the key!

So if you see signs that make you chuckle,
Embrace the odd paths, let luck be your struggle.
For on this wild ride, joy reigns supreme,
And life is just better with a wacky dream!

## The Hidden Trail of Hope

In a forest of laughter, a path does appear,
Made of bright clovers, it brings forth cheer.
With each little step, there's a joke to be found,
A ticklish tick-tock as we dance around!

Oh, look there! A gopher with a fedora so fine,
He's throwing a party, with snacks and wine!
Come join the fun, the joy, the surprise,
With clovers as decorations, oh, what a prize!

But wait, a snail steals the peak of the cake,
With frosting all over, for goodness' sake!
We laugh and we giggle, our troubles depart,
For silly little moments can warm the heart.

As we wander this trail, hand in hand,
With giggles and clovers scattered like sand.
Hope blooms around in every bright hue,
In this zany adventure, we find something new!

## Beneath a Canopy of Fortune

Under a canopy twisted with cheer,
Fortune hides laughter, come gather here.
Each clover a treasure, so small yet grand,
Ready for giggles, just take my hand!

Underneath leaves that giggle and sway,
A troupe of ants puts on quite a play.
Their tiny ballet with acorn caps,
Leaves us all laughing, falling in laps!

A tiny toad croaks a tune of delight,
Inviting the moon to join in the night.
With whispers of wishes on breezes so light,
This canopy glows, oh what a sight!

So grab a clover, don't let it roam,
Funny little fortunes will lead you home.
In this cheerful wonderland, luck is a dance,
With smiles and laughter in each little chance!

www.ingramcontent.com/pod-product-compliance
Lightning Source LLC
Chambersburg PA
CBHW071837160426
43209CB00003B/327